Around the World in 32 Teeth

A boy's journey to discover what to do with his tooth

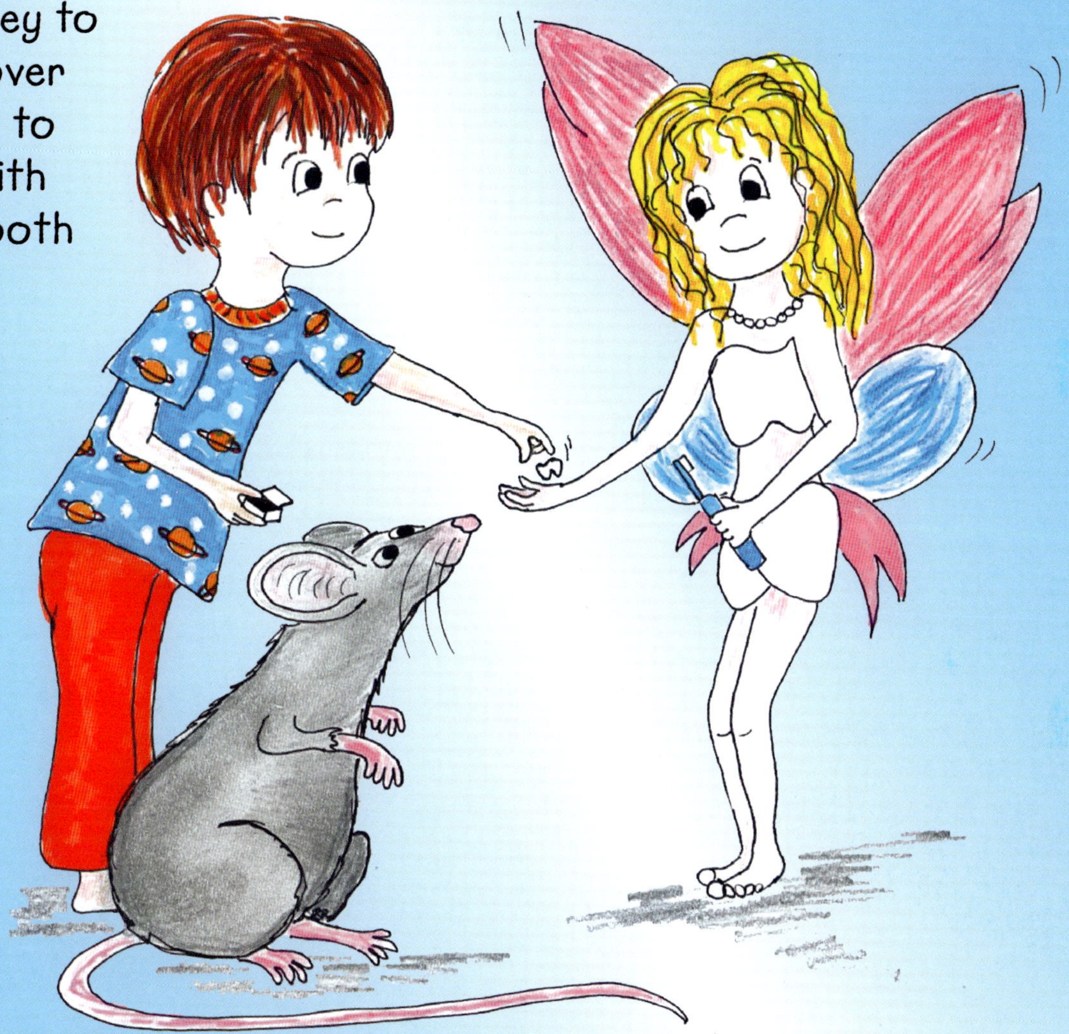

Written by Olympia Filippeli

Illustrated by Ranan Richardson

Seattle, Washington
Portland, Oregon
Denver, Colorado
Vancouver, B.C.
Scottsdale, Arizona
Minneapolis, Minnesota

ISBN: 978-1-59849-071-8
Library of Congress Control Number: 2009904727

Printed in China by Global PSD

A special thanks to Amalia Decca
Design: Soundview Design Studio

Peanut Butter Publishing
2925 Fairview Avenue East
Seattle, Washington 98102
877-728-8837
www.peanutbutterpublishing.com

To my beloved Mother

I dedicate this book
for always being there
for me
and for providing the
magic in my world.

It is a pleasure and an honor for me to write a few words about Olympia Filippeli's wonderful book *Around the World in 32 Teeth.*

Beginning with a child's agony about losing a baby tooth- something we have all experienced – the book's title character, Jamie, takes us to 32 different countries around the world and, in doing so, underscores the importance of some of humanity's greatest ideals, including diversity, equality, respect and mutual understanding. It is heartening to know that, in today's difficult times, there are teenagers like author Olympia Filippeli, who realize the importance of getting along and sharing with each other the different traditions and cultures across the globe that are a part of who we are.

I am proud to introduce you to such a well-written and meaningful book. I believe that children and adults alike will find it entertaining and informative. Enjoy Jamie's journey!

Daniel V. Speckhard
U.S. Ambassador to Greece

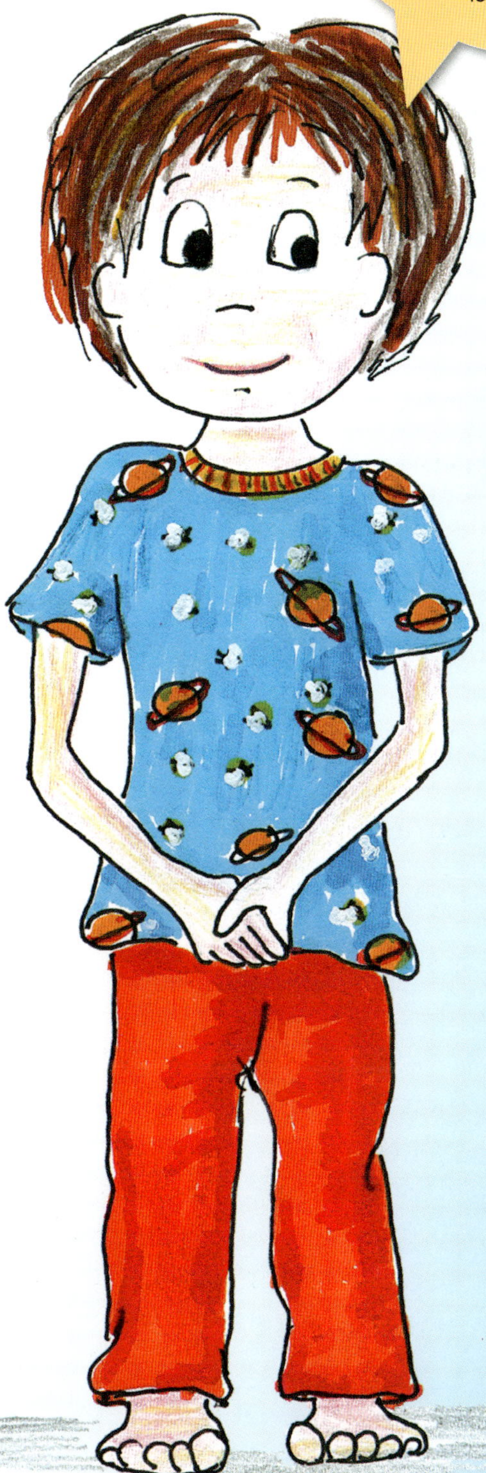

Jamie has a similar problem.

You see, he lost his tooth, but not just any tooth.

His first tooth.

Do you remember when you lost your first tooth?

What did you do next?

And if you haven't lost one yet, what will you do when you lose that one?

Well, Jamie's family came to America six years ago from sunny Greece. In Greece when you lose your tooth, you throw it onto the roof, but in America you wait for the Tooth Fairy. So what should Jamie do?

"Mummy, what should I do with my tooth?" Jamie asked.

"Why, throw it onto the roof dear!" replied his mother.

"But, Mummy, my friends in school say I should wait for the Tooth Fairy like they do," exclaimed Jamie.

"But you are Greek my dear, and in Greece we throw it onto the roof. However, if you want to wait for the Tooth Fairy you can. Whatever you want," she said in an understanding voice.

That night Jamie didn't know what to do. He lay in his bed with his tooth in his hand, wondering. He could follow his Greek tradition and throw it onto the roof, but what if the Tooth Fairy came, and she didn't find his tooth? That would make her upset, wouldn't it? Slowly, slowly as the night fell Jamie started to fall asleep, and then wonderful dreams came to mind.

Big lush valleys, rainbows with golden pots at the end, and bunny-shaped clouds everywhere. Beautiful, wonderful dreams. Then suddenly, something woke him up. It was still night outside, but his tooth had slipped from his hand and fallen onto the floor. This smell in the air, what was it? Something like fresh mint, with fruits inside. Toothpaste!!! That's it! Toothpaste, thought Jamie. But why would he smell toothpaste in the middle of the night? Suddenly he heard a faint noise, like wings flapping and then sparkles, bright blue and white sparkles, and then out of nowhere

there she was. Carried by two white, shiny teeth with wings and one big tooth that she sat in, there she was whiter than white and sparkly clear. The Tooth Fairy!!

Beautiful, wonderful dreams...

She looked very young, almost like Jamie's age; however, he recognized her immediately, mostly because of what she was wearing, which looked like two teeth as a shirt and a dress facing each other upside down.

"Hello Jamie, do you know who I am?" she said in a soft voice.

"The Tooth Fairy," replied Jamie.

"Very good Jamie", she exclaimed. "I heard you wondering in the night. So you don't know what to do with your tooth?"

"My friends say to give it to you, but my Mummy says that I should throw it on the roof. What should I do? And which one is right?" Jamie asked.

"My dear, Jamie, there is no such thing as wrong or right when it comes to traditions. When your Mummy was a young girl, she threw her tooth on the roof. That's why she is telling you to do the same thing," replied the tooth fairy softly.

"So people don't give their tooth only to you?" asked Jamie, surprised.

"But of course not. I have many other friends that do the same job I do, and we all help each other. Just as your Mummy is a teacher, there are many other people who are teachers too. There are many different traditions around the world that kids just like you follow when they lose their tooth."

"Like what kinds of traditions?" Jamie asked eagerly.

"Why don't you come with me and I'll show you. You can also meet my friends," offered the tooth fairy.

"I would love that!" said Jamie.

"But before we do all that, Jamie, you are too big to fit in my carriage, so in order to become small like me, you must repeat exactly what I say. Can you do that, Jamie?", asked the tooth fairy.

"I think so," said Jamie.

"All right then, repeat after me three times: Brush your teeth three times a day, and that will keep the dentist away", said the tooth fairy.

"Brush your teeth three times a day, and that will keep the dentist away," repeated Jamie once.

"Brush your teeth three times a day, and that will keep the dentist away," repeated Jamie twice.

"Brush your teeth three times a day, and that will keep the dentist away," repeated Jamie three times.

"Poof!" sparkles in the air, the smell of toothpaste stronger than ever, and Jamie was standing there next to the Tooth Fairy. However, something was different. She was the exact size he was, but how did she grow so fast? Then suddenly, he looked around and saw that the room had gotten so big, and his bed was huge. It wasn't the Tooth Fairy who had grown, but he who had become really, really small.

"Are you ready?" asked the Tooth Fairy.

"Yes", replied Jamie, still a bit shocked.

So they jumped in her carriage pulled by the two teeth with wings, and off they went, leaving behind them a scent of mint.

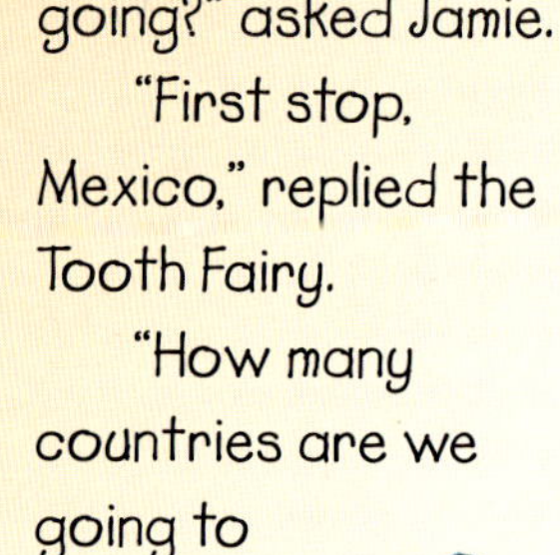

"Where are we going?" asked Jamie.

"First stop, Mexico," replied the Tooth Fairy.

"How many countries are we going to visit?" asked Jamie.

"Thirty-two, one for every tooth", answered the Tooth Fairy.

"Wow!" said Jamie.

"Hola, Tooth Fairy," said a mouse coming near them.

"Hola, El Raton. Jamie, I want you to meet my friend El Raton. El Raton, this is Jamie. I am taking him around the world to show him what all the other kids do with their teeth when they lose them," she said.

"Hola, Jamie! In Mexico, kids leave their tooth under their pillow or in a box for me to take," said El Raton.

"El Raton has many cousins that help him do the same job that I do all over the world," exclaimed the tooth fairy.

"Yes, we are a big family. Come let me show you," said the mouse politely.

"We are going to make a small stop in Costa Rica, country number two, since it is on our way," said El Raton.

"Hola, cousin," said El Raton. "Jamie, this is El Raton Miguelito. We are showing Jamie the different tooth traditions."

"Hello", said Jamie.

"Hello, my dear boy. In Costa Rica kids put their tooth under the pillow so I can come and get it. After I take the tooth, I leave them some money, so I can thank them for giving me their tooth," said El Raton Miguelito.

"Just like the Tooth Fairy does!!" exclaimed Jamie.

"Just like me. Now time to move on. Next stop, Colombia, country number three," exclaimed El Raton.

"Hola, Roza!" said the Tooth Fairy.

"Hello", said the little girl.

"What do you do with your tooth when you lose it?" asked Jamie.

"We dip it in silver or in gold and wear it as an earring," said the girl.

"Thank you," said Jamie.

"Next stop Argentina, country number four," said the Tooth Fairy.

"Hola, my cousin," shouted El Raton.

"El Raton! How I've missed you," the second mouse shouted back.

"Jamie, this is El Raton's cousin, El Ratoncito. We are showing Jamie the different tooth traditions all over the world."

"Hello, Jamie. Here in Argentina, most children put their tooth in a glass of water for me. So once I get there all thirsty, I get to drink the water and take the tooth," El Ratoncito said.

"That's very nice of them" said Jamie.

"Yes, indeed. Next stop, country number five, Spain," said the Tooth Fairy.

"This is my favorite city," said El Raton. "Now where is my cousin?"

"Is that him?" asked Jamie, seeing a mouse approaching them.

"Yes! Hola, my cousin. Jamie, this is my cousin El Ratoncito Perrez. Dear cousin, we are showing Jamie the different tooth traditions all over the world," said El Raton.

"Hola, Jamie. In Spain, children put their tooth under their pillow so I can come and get it, and in return I leave them some money to thank them for giving me their tooth."

"Time to go. Adios, El Ratoncito Perrez," said El Raton.

"Next stop, country number six, France," said the Tooth Fairy.

A Paris...

"Salut, my cousin," shouted El Raton.

"Salut, El Raton," said the mouse.

"This is Jamie. We are showing him the different tooth traditions all over the world. Jamie, this is my cousin La Petite Souris."

"Hello, Jamie. In France, children leave their tooth under their pillow for me to take, and in return I give them a present," said La Petite Souris.

"Interesting," said Jamie.

"Yes, it is. Au revoir, La Petite Souris. We must go. Next stop, Russia, country number seven", said the Tooth Fairy.

"This is where most of my family lives, but because it gets so cold and it snows a lot, most of them live underground," El Raton said.

"El Raton, over here," shouted a mouse while climbing out of a hole.

"Zdrasvetya, cousin, this is Jamie. We are showing him the different tooth traditions all over the world," said El Raton

"Sounds very interesting. Well, in Russia children drop their tooth in the holes in the ground that lead to our houses, or they leave them out so we can come and get them," said the mouse.

"And what do you do with all those teeth in your house?" asked Jamie.

"We use them as chairs, and beds, and other furniture," said the mouse.

"Well, Jamie, I have to leave you both now as I have a lot of relatives to visit here in Russia. But have fun on the rest of your trip" said El Raton.

"Thanks so much, El Raton, for introducing me to all your family. It was very nice to meet you", said Jamie sadly.

"It was nice meeting you too, Jamie. Bye bye," replied El Raton.

"Next stop, country number eight, Greece" said the Tooth Fairy excitedly.

"Geia sou, Stavros, this is Jamie," said the Tooth Fairy

"Hello," replied Stavros.

"I'm showing Jamie all the different tooth traditions around the world. What do you do with your tooth?" asked the Tooth Fairy.

"Well, I throw it onto the roof," replied Stavros.

"Just like my mummy did when she was a little girl," exclaimed Jamie.

"Next stop, Romania, country number nine," said the Tooth Fairy.

"Salut, Camelia," said the Tooth Fairy.

"Hello," replied the girl.

"What do you do with your tooth?" asked Jamie.

"I throw it onto the roof saying, Crow, crow, take this iron tooth and bring me a steel one," replied Camelia.

"Cool," said Jamie.

"Next stop, Germany, country number ten," said the Tooth Fairy.

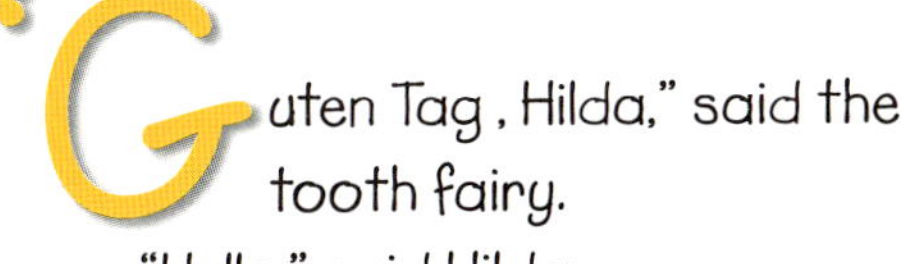

"Guten Tag , Hilda," said the tooth fairy.

"Hello," said Hilda.

"What do you do with your tooth?" asked Jamie.

"I wait for her to take it and give me some money," Hilda answered pointing at the fairy.

"Thanks," replied Jamie.

"Next stop, country number eleven, Denmark," said the Tooth Fairy.

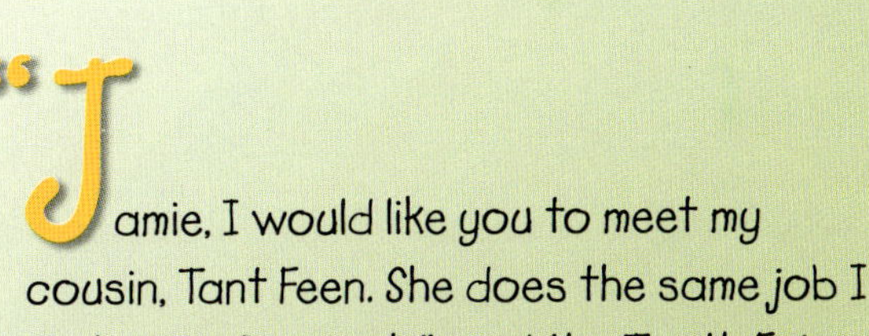

"Jamie, I would like you to meet my cousin, Tant Feen. She does the same job I do here in Denmark," said the Tooth Fairy.

"Goddag, Jamie. Nice to meet you," said Tant Feen.

"Nice to meet you too," replied Jamie. What do the Danes do with their teeth? The children here do the same thing as in Germany. They put it under their pillow and wait for me to come . "Wow, two countries so close and even the same traditions." exclaimed Jamie.

"Next stop, country number twelve, Mali" said the Tooth Fairy.

"I be di, Neo", said the Tooth Fairy.

"Hello," said the boy.

"What do you do with your tooth?" asked Jamie.

"Well, I throw it into a chicken house, and the next day a chicken will be there in its place for us to eat," exclaimed the boy.

"Thank you," said Jamie.

"Next stop, country number thirteen, Senegal," said the Tooth Fairy.

"Bonjour, Simba," said the Tooth Fairy.

"Hello," said the boy.

"What do you do with your tooth?" asked Jamie.

"I throw it into a river so a fish can come and take it and bring me a new one" replied Simba.

"That's interesting" said Jamie.

"Next stop, country number fourteen, Nigeria," said the Tooth Fairy.

"How now, Zuri", said the Tooth Fairy.

"Hello," said the girl.

"What do you do with your tooth?" asked Jamie.

"Well, because I am a girl, I hold my tooth in one hand with six stones, so with the tooth it makes seven, and then I close my eyes and say my name out loud. Then I count to the number of stones and teeth I have in my hand and throw them and run away saying, I want my tooth back. Boys hold eight stones with their tooth, which makes nine," replied Zuri.

"Next stop, country number fifteen, Botswana," said the Tooth Fairy.

"Dumela, Oni," said the tooth fairy.

"Hello," said Oni.

"What do you do with your tooth?" asked Jamie.

"In Botswana, we throw it onto the roof and ask the moon to bring us a new one", said Oni.

"That's neat," said Jamie.

"Next stop, country number sixteen, South Africa," said the Tooth Fairy.

"Hallo, Ama," said the Tooth Fairy.

"Hello," said the girl.

"What do you do with your tooth?" asked Jamie.

"In South Africa, we put it in a slipper, and a mouse comes and takes it."

"I wonder if that mouse is one of El Raton's cousins?" Jamie said.

"Maybe, they are a big family," replied the Tooth Fairy.

"Next stop, country number seventeen, Madagascar."

"Salama, Ashanti", said the Tooth Fairy.

"Hello," said Ashanti.

"What do you do with your tooth?" asked Jamie.

"I throw it on the roof of the house or a neighbor's house saying, Here is my bad tooth. I want a new one," replied Ashanti.

"Next stop, country number eighteen, Tanzania" said the Tooth Fairy.

"Salama, Femi," said the Tooth Fairy.

"Hello," said Femi.

"What do you do with your tooth?" asked Jamie.

"In Tanzania, we throw the tooth over the roof, sometimes facing forward sometimes facing backwards, saying, Dear crow, take this bad tooth and give me a good white one," replied Femi.

"Thank you," said Jamie.

"Next stop, country nineteen, Egypt," said the Tooth Fairy.

"Salaam, Hanan," said the Tooth Fairy.

"Hello," said the girl.

""What do you do with your tooth?" asked Jamie.

"In Egypt, we wrap the tooth in cloth and throw it as high as we can to Ra, the sun god, saying, Shiny sun, shiny sun, take this buffalo's tooth and bring me a bride's tooth," replied the girl.

"Thank you" said Jamie.

"Next stop, country number twenty, Pakistan" said the Tooth Fairy.

"Salaam, Abia," said the Tooth Fairy.

"Hello," said Abia.

"What do you do with your tooth in Pakistan?" asked Jamie.

"I wrap my tooth in a piece of cotton or cloth and bury it in the garden or throw it into the river. If we are not close to water, we bury it," replied Abia.

"Interesting, thank you," said Jamie.

"Next stop, country number twenty-one, India," said the Tooth Fairy.

"Namaste, Lila," said the tooth fairy to the small sparrow.

"Hello," said Lila.

"What do the kids in India do with their tooth?" asked Jamie.

"They throw it onto the roof and ask me to bring them a new one" chirped Lila.

"Thank you" replied Jamie politely.

"Next stop, country number twenty-two, Sri Lanka," said the Tooth Fairy.

"Aaybovan, Jay," said the Tooth Fairy to a squirrel.

"Hello," said Jay.

"What do the kids in Sri Lanka do when they lose their first tooth?" asked Jamie.

"They throw it onto the roof for me to come and get it saying, May I get strong, milky white teeth thereafter."

"That's neat" said Jamie.

"Next stop, country number twenty-three, Malaysia," said the Tooth Fairy.

"Namaskkaram, Jaafar," said the Tooth Fairy.

"Hello," said Jaafar.

"What do you do with your tooth?" asked Jamie.

"In Malaysia, we believe that since our tooth is a part of us, it must be buried in the ground to return to earth, just as we will one day," replied Jaafar.

"Very interesting. Thank you", said Jamie.

"You're welcome," replied Jaafar.

"Next stop, country twenty-four, Thailand," said the Tooth Fairy.

"Sawatdi, Jaidee," said the Tooth Fairy.

"Hello," said Jaidee.

"What do you do with your tooth?" asked Jamie.

"In Thailand, if it's the upper tooth, we bury it in the ground, and if it's the lower tooth, we throw it onto the roof," said Jaidee.

"Thank you," said Jamie.

"Next stop, country number twenty-five, Bhutan," said the Tooth Fairy.

"Yala, Moe," said the Tooth Fairy.

"Hello," said Moe.

"What do you do with your tooth?" asked Jamie.

"I throw it onto the roof as an offering to the Moon Goddess, and she will grant me a good, strong, new tooth," replied Moe.

"That's cool," said Jamie.

"Next stop, country number twenty-six, Nepal" said the Tooth Fairy.

"Namaste, Hina," said the Tooth Fairy.

"Hello," said Hina.

"What do kids do in Nepal with their lost tooth?" asked Jamie.

"We have many traditions in Nepal. We bury our tooth in the garden or in cow poop, or we throw it onto the roof."

"Thank you," said Jamie.

"Next stop, country number twenty-seven, China," said the Tooth Fairy.

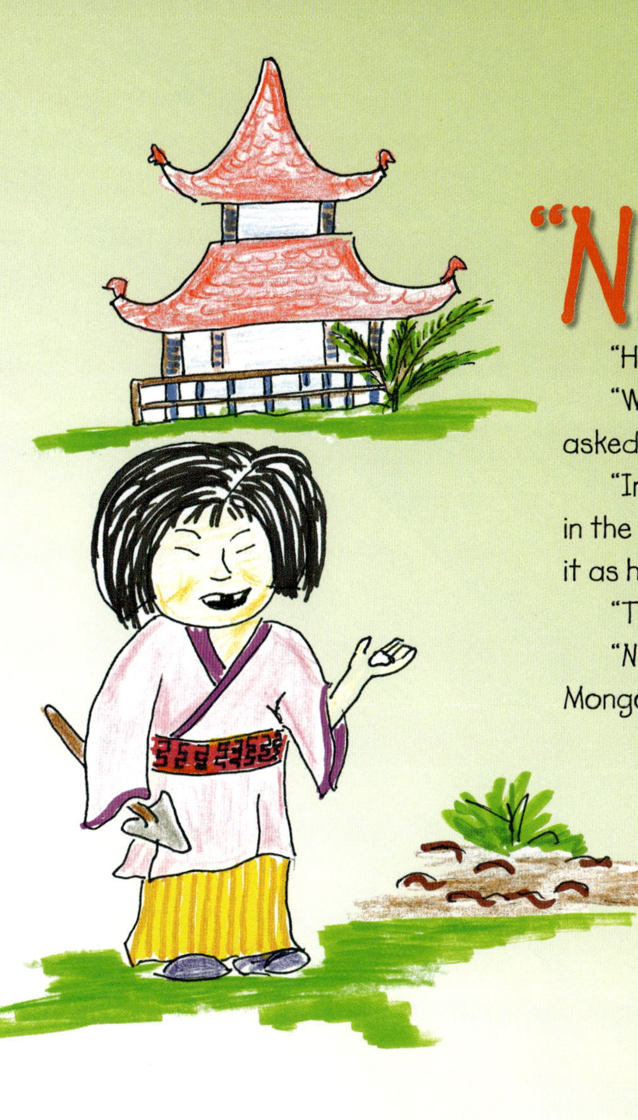

"Néih hóu, Song" said the tooth fairy.

"Hello", replied Song.

"What do you do with your tooth?" asked Jamie.

"In China, if it's the upper tooth, we bury it in the ground, if it's the lower tooth, we throw it as high as we can to the sky," replied Song.

"Thank you," said Jamie.

"Next stop, country number twenty- eight, Mongolia," exclaimed the Tooth Fairy.

"Sain baina uu, Kushi," said the Tooth Fairy to the big white dog.

"Hello," said Kushi.

"What do kids in Mongolia do with their teeth when they fall out?" asked Jamie.

"Well they wrap it in delicious fat and give it to me to eat. Then they ask to me to bring them a new healthy tooth," said Kushi.

"Wow, that's very different from what we do," said Jamie.

"Yes, indeed. Next stop, country number twenty-nine, Korea, " said the Tooth Fairy.

"Annyong, Min Ki," said the Tooth Fairy.

"Hello," said Min Ki.

"What do kids in Korea do with their lost tooth?" asked Jamie.

"When I loose my tooth, I stand on a balcony and sing a song that tells the birds that I'll give them my old tooth in return for a new tooth. Then I close my eyes and throw it into the air," replied Min Ki.

"Thank you very much," said Jamie.

"Next stop, country number thirty, the Philippines," said the Tooth Fairy.

"Halo, Rowena," said the Tooth Fairy.

"Hello" said Rowena.

"What do you do with your lost tooth, Rowena?" asked Jamie.

"I bury it in the ground, and if I can find it next year, then I get to make another wish," said Rowena.

"Interesting", said Jamie.

Next stop, country number thirty-one, Australia," said the Tooth Fairy.

"Now where's my cousin?" said the Tooth Fairy.

"Wow, Australia! Now we are really far away from home," exclaimed Jamie.

"There she is!" said the Tooth Fairy, pointing to another fairy that looked very much like her, who was standing next to a girl with bright red hair.

"Hallo, cousin" said the Tooth Fairy's cousin.

"Jamie, this is my cousin. Cousin, this is Jamie and he is wondering what the kids in Australia do with their lost tooth." "Well, Jamie, why don't you ask Audrey who lives in Australia what she does with her tooth," answered the Tooth Fairy's cousin, pointing to the red-headed girl next to her.

"Hey, Audrey, what do you do when you lose your tooth?" asked Jamie.

"I put it under my pillow, and the Tooth Fairy comes and takes it and leaves me some money," answered Audrey.

"Wow," said Jamie. "That's exactly what I do. Its weird how we live so far away, but we have the same tradition."

"Yes," agreed Audrey.

"Well, Jamie", said the Tooth Fairy, "now we are headed back to where we started from. Next and last stop, country number thirty-two, home sweet home, America. This is where I get to take children's lost teeth and give them some money in return."

As Jamie was arriving home, he was thinking of all the different traditions he saw and how many things he learned in one night. He had travelled the whole world just in one night. How amazing was that?

"Thank you very much" Jamie said to the Tooth Fairy. "I had so much fun and learned so many things".

"You're welcome, Jamie. Now you know that there are many different traditions in the world and that there is no such thing as a wrong tradition. You are free to follow whichever one you want," exclaimed the Tooth Fairy.

"Yes, but I still don't know which one to follow," said Jamie.

"In time you will, Jamie. Just do what your heart tells you," she said.

"And now, repeat after me three times so you can return to your normal size: Brush your teeth three times a day, and that will keep the dentist away." "Brush your teeth three times a day, and that will keep the dentist away," repeated Jamie once.

"Brush your teeth three times a day, and that will keep the dentist away," repeated Jamie twice.

"Brush your teeth three times a day, and that will keep the dentist away" repeated Jamie three times, and with a loud "bang" he returned to his original size.

"I must go now. Good bye, Jamie," said the Tooth Fairy.

"I will miss you and thank you so much for sharing all these interesting traditions with me. I would never have known. Good-bye", said Jamie.

"You're welcome, Jamie. Just remember, follow your heart's desires," she said and with a sudden sprinkle of blue and white sparkles, she disappeared, leaving behind her a fresh smell of mint tooth paste.

It was only then that Jamie realized how tired he was. Closing his eyes, he lay back and quickly fell asleep.

“Jamie, dear, wake up”, said Jamie's mother.

Jamie slowly opened his eyes and memories of his trip passed through his mind. Was it just a dream? Or did that all really happen? As he was getting ready for school, he couldn't stop thinking if he really went to all those places last night. But suddenly, as he picked up his bag he found a tooth, not his tooth, but a tooth like the one the tooth fairy wore.

“So it was real” he said to himself.

When he arrived at school, he told all his friends of all the different traditions. His friends got so interested that they decided to follow different traditions also. So, when school ended they all went to the river, and some threw their tooth in, some threw it into the air, some onto a roof nearby for the sun or the sparrow or the crow to come get it, some left it in a cup of water for El Ratoncito to come, and some buried it in the ground. Jamie, however left it for the Tooth Fairy with a note saying:

"Dear Tooth Fairy,
Please take this tooth to Greece and throw it onto a roof for me.

Miss you,
Love, Jamie".

About the Author
Olympia-Sophia Filippeli

Two great factors have determined the course of my being. An American mother and a Greek father. Growing up in multicultural environment, I had the chance to learn that there is more than one tradition and above all that they are all correct and unique in their own way.

At the age of 15, I used my 10th grade school project for acceptance into the IB program to put my dream on paper. My mother used to be a tour guide, so I had the opportunity to grow up surrounded by the many traditions she had learned on her way around the world. I decided to put all these traditions that I had learned about what children do with when they loose their first teeth into book form. Since my dream has always been to become an author, I thought that this would be the perfect start, and it might even help me finance my way through university. I wrote to all the national tourist organizations around the world to confirm that the stories my mom had told me were true. I also researched how to say hello in every country, along with the most popular names, so each child coming from those countries I chose would identify with my story. The reason I choose 32 countries was because we have 32 teeth, but we must not forget that there are so many other countries with their unique traditions that unfortunately it wasn't possible to include them all. Our web site www.olympiasophi.com will offer for those who are interested more information about the countries mentioned along with the many others around the world. I hope you enjoy reading this book as much as I have creating it.

About the Illustrator
Ranan Richardson

Having given up my pen and pencils and colored crayons since my transient days as a tour guide, it always surprises me what can be created by pure, unadulterated motherly love.

"In our American-centric view, it's very important for our youth to understand and appreciate other customs surrounding the universal childhood experience of loosing teeth. Olympia's prose and Ranan's artistry bring to life this magical trip with the Tooth Fairy to a myriad of countries. This book is perfect for school and home libraries to help foster discussions about world cultures, dental health and, most importantly, the magical lose of the first tooth."

Dr. Terence K. McAteer
Inyo County Superintendent of Schools, California

"Children are the future of the world and as adults we have an obligation to provide them with the tools they need to become responsible citizens. As parents we provide our children with a harmonious life and the sense of tradition. Olympia's tender story of childhood dilemma that most of us face is a moving reminder that we all have a custom to share in this small world. Weaving together questions that children worldwide have such as what to do when one loses a tooth gives Olympia the opportunity to take us on a thrilling trip to our youthful roots where sometimes solutions could be found in the most innovative and exciting way. It is refreshing to see a young person like Olympia undertaking such a wonderful endeavor in sharing her thoughts and love for children with us.

Stefanos Gialamas, Ph.D.
President, American Community
Schools of Athens